1986

W9-BHL-190

DEAR JOSHUA!

MERRY CHRISTMAS
&
HAPPY READING

LOVE

OMA & OPA.

Animals Around Us

Animals of the Seashore
Animals of the Fields and Meadows
Animals of the Woods and Forests
Animals of the Ponds and Streams

Animals of the Fields and Meadows

by
Julie Becker

EMC Publishing, St. Paul, Minnesota

to
Northfield
the way it was

Library of Congress Cataloging in Publication Data

Becker, Julie
   Animals of the fields and meadows.

   Includes Index
   (Her Animals around us)
   SUMMARY: Describes ten animals, such as the red-
tailed hawk, garter snake, and cottontail rabbit, that
live in fields and meadows
   1. Meadow fauna—Juvenile literature. [1. Meadow
animals] I. Roth-Evenson, Maarja. II. Title.
III. Series.
QL115.5.B4   591.5'264   77-8496
   ISBN 0-88436-394-5

Copyright 1977, 1982 by EMC Corporation
All rights reserved. Published 1977.
Revised Edition 1982.

No part of this publication may be
reproduced, stored in a retrieval
system, or transmitted in any form
or by any means; electronic, mechanical,
photocopying, recording, or otherwise,
without the permission of the publisher.

Published by EMC Publishing
180 East Sixth Street
St. Paul, Minnesota 55101
Printed in the United States of America
0 9 8 7 6 5 4 3 2

TABLE OF CONTENTS

Fields and Meadows

Fields and meadows are in open places. Tall grass and tall weeds grow in the fields and meadows. Pink and yellow and blue flowers add color to the fields and meadows. Bees buzz, crickets chirp and birds sing beautiful songs.

Many animals live in the fields and meadows. Some spin webs. Some hide under the grass. And some fly in the air. Some eat grass and weeds. Some drink juice from flowers. And some eat meat.

Go for a walk in the fields and meadows. Hunt for animals in the morning. Hunt for animals at night. See how many animals you can find.

The Cricket

It is summer. It is dark outside. The night has come. The fields are full of music. The crickets are singing.

The male cricket sings for the female cricket. He likes to chirp to her. He likes to make music for her.

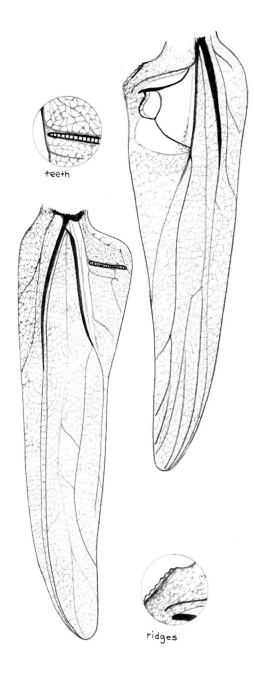

teeth

ridges

He makes music with his wings. He has little teeth on his wings. He has little ridges on his wings too. The teeth are on the bottom of his wings. The ridges are on the top of his wings.

The cricket puts one wing on top of the other. He rubs his wings together. He saws back and forth. The teeth on his wings rub over the little ridges. He looks like he is playing the fiddle. This is how he sings. This is how he chirps.

The female cricket can not sing. Female crickets do not have teeth on their wings. They do not have ridges on their wings. But a female cricket can hear. She can hear the male's song. She can hear him when he plays his fiddle.

Crickets do not have ears on their heads. They have ears on their front legs. They have ears on their knees. Both the male cricket and the female cricket can hear very well. The sounds in the air come right to their knees. This is how they hear.

10

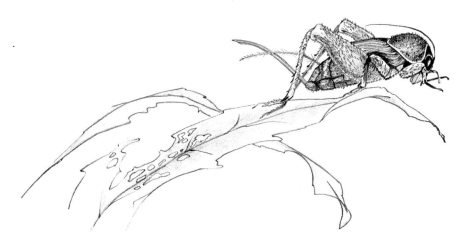

A cricket has six legs. His back legs are big. They are made for jumping. A cricket likes to jump and hop. He likes to jump and hop in the fields. Sometimes it is hard to catch a cricket. He jumps right out of your hands.

A cricket likes to eat a lot. He likes to bite on little plants. He likes to eat seeds. He likes to eat grass. He likes to eat fruit and vegetables.

Sometimes farmers get mad at crickets. Crickets eat their beans and their peas. Crickets eat their wheat and their oats. Crickets eat the food in their fields.

Many crickets live in the fields. Some are black and some are brown. It is not very hard to find one. Turn over an old log. Turn over a rock. You may see one or two crickets hiding on the ground.

The Cottontail Rabbit

The cottontail rabbit sits in the tall grass. Her ears stick up straight. Her eyes open wide. Her nose wiggles up and down.

It is early in the morning. The cottontail rabbit wants to eat her breakfast. But she has to be very careful. Big animals like to chase rabbits. They like to eat rabbits. So the rabbit's eyes and ears and nose will tell her if she is safe.

Her big eyes bulge out. They are on the side of her head. She can see in front and in back at the same time. She can look all ways.

Her nose wiggles. Her tall ears move around. If a fox is walking in the fields, she will hear him. She will smell him. She will sit very quietly. She will hide.

If a fox sees her, she will run away. Her back legs are strong. They are made for running and jumping. They work like big strong springs. They push her into the air.

The rabbit will run fast. The fox will chase her. The rabbit will run in circles. She will run in zigzags. She will try to fool the fox.

If the rabbit is lucky, she will get away. She will jump under a bush. She will hide under some tall grass. The fox will not be able to find her. The tall grass is light brown. The rabbit's fur is light brown too. It is hard to see the rabbit when she hides in the tall grass.

The rabbit comes out to eat when she is safe. She eats early in the morning or late in the afternoon. She likes to eat vegetables. She likes to eat grass and flowers and weeds. She loves to eat clover!

A rabbit has big front teeth. She nibbles on clover with her big front teeth. If you watch a rabbit eat, you can see her big teeth in front. You can see two big teeth on the top and two big teeth on the bottom. She bites her vegetables with her big teeth.

The rabbit also has two extra teeth in front. Her two extra teeth are behind her two top teeth. She really has four long teeth on the top. Her extra teeth help her to bite and nibble. If a rabbit opens her mouth wide, you can see her extra teeth.

The rabbit's long teeth are like your fingernails. They are always growing. She bites on plants. She bites on bark. But her teeth do not wear down. As long as the rabbit lives, her teeth will grow.

The rabbit has flat teeth in the back of her mouth. She grinds up her food with her flat teeth. She always grinds up her food well before she swallows it.

The cottontail rabbit has a lot of babies in the summer. Before she has her babies, she makes a nest. She makes her nest in the tall grass. She pulls soft fur from her belly. She puts her soft fur in the middle of her nest. She wants her babies to be warm.

At first, her babies will be very tiny. Each baby will be about as big as a mouse. The babies will not have any fur. Their eyes will not be open. The mother cottontail will feed the tiny babies. She will feed them milk.

Soon the babies will open their eyes. They will grow fur. They will have little white cottontails like their mother. When they are two weeks old, they will find their own food. They will nibble on little plants.

The mother rabbit will watch her babies. She will help to keep them safe. If a fox is coming, the mother rabbit thumps her back foot on the ground. This tells her babies to run and hide.

If you walk in the fields, you may not see a rabbit. Rabbits are afraid of you. Rabbits will hide from you. But one day, you may be lucky. You may be walking down the road late in the afternoon. You may see a light brown rabbit hopping quickly across the field.

The Garter Snake

The black and yellow garter snake slides quietly along the ground. He slides in and out of the tall grass. His thin red tongue slips in and out of his mouth.

Some people think that the snake can sting with his tongue. But this is not true. He smells with his tongue. He tastes the air with his tongue. His tongue will not hurt you.

You like to eat food three times a day. But the garter snake only eats once a week. He likes to eat meat. He likes to eat worms. He likes to eat small frogs.

A snake has many little teeth. His teeth feel like little pins. They grow in rows. They bend back. They bend back towards his throat.

The garter snake can grab with his teeth. He can grab a small frog. But he can not chew the frog with his teeth. His teeth are too small. He can not chew his food at all. He swallows his food whole.

A snake has a thin body. A frog has a fat body. But the snake can swallow the frog whole. The snake has special jaws. His jaws are not wide. But they can stretch.

You have two jaws. Your jaws are held together. They are held together with tight strings.

The snake has two jaws too. His jaws are held together. But his jaw strings are not tight. His jaw strings are like rubber bands. If the snake wants to swallow something big, his jaws stretch.

After the snake swallows the frog, he looks funny. He has a big bump in his body. His skin has to stretch. The frog is inside of him. The skin stretches so the frog will fit.

Some people think snakes are wet and slippery. But snakes are really dry. A snake has scales all over his body. The scales help him move. The scales hold on to the ground. The snake has no legs. But he can move just as fast as you can!

Every summer, the garter snake gets a new skin. His old skin begins to look dry and gray. The skin around his mouth cracks. He rubs against a stone. He wiggles out of his old skin. He leaves his old skin behind. The colors on his new skin look very bright.

If you walk in the field, you might find an old snake skin. The snake skin will not have any color. Pick up the old skin. You can see the shape of the snake's eyes. You can see the shape of all his scales.

Look for garter snakes in the fields. Pick up a garter snake. Hold him behind his head so he can not bite. Watch his red tongue move in and out of his mouth. Feel his scales. Then let him go. Let him slide in and out of the grass. Let him rest in the warm sun.

The Meadowlark

The male meadowlark sits on the fence. He sings a happy song. The sun is shining. The meadowlark's bright yellow breast looks beautiful in the sunshine.

The female meadowlark is in the field. She is not as easy to see. The brown feathers on her back match the color of the dry grass in the field. The yellow feathers on her breast are not very bright.

The female meadowlark listens to the male's song. She makes a nest in the field. Her nest will be on the ground. She makes her nest out of dry grass. She puts soft grass and horse hairs inside of her nest. She wants her nest to be warm and comfortable.

The meadowlark makes a roof for her nest. She makes her roof out of grass. If it rains, her nest will not get wet. She and her babies will stay dry.

There will be one little door in the meadowlark's nest. The door will be on the side of the nest. A secret path will go up to the door. The path will be covered with grass.

The meadowlark lays four, five or six eggs. When the eggs hatch, the young babies stay in the nest. When the babies get older, they will learn how to walk. They will learn how to walk on the secret path.

Meadowlarks have long, strong legs. They have big feet. They walk when they hunt for food. They do not run or hop. The baby meadowlarks have to learn how to walk well. They will walk a lot when they get big.

The meadowlark has a long bill. Her bill is pointed. She pokes on the ground with her bill. She hunts for food. She likes to eat grasshoppers and crickets. She likes to eat beetles.

Both the male meadowlark and the female meadowlark take care of their babies. They find food for the babies. They bring insects to the babies. The mother and the father and the babies all live in the fields together.

Most farmers like meadowlarks. Meadowlarks eat insects that can hurt the farmer's plants. Meadowlarks help the farmers. So be careful when you run in a farmer's field. Watch where you step. A family of meadowlarks may be hiding under the long tall grass.

The Spider

Many people are afraid of spiders. They think spiders are ugly. They think spiders will hurt them.

But most spiders do not hurt people. They do not bite people. They want to eat insects. They want to eat grasshoppers and flies.

A lot of spiders spin webs. They spin webs on flowers and plants. They spin webs on trees. They spin webs on the ground. But some spiders do not spin webs at all.

The crab spider is a spider who has no web. A crab spider hides in flowers. It is very hard to see a crab spider. If a crab spider hides in a yellow flower, she will turn yellow. If a crab spider hides in a white flower, she will turn white.

The crab spider can catch insects with her long front legs. She hides in a flower. She stays very quiet. She waits for an insect. When an insect lands on the flower, the crab spider grabs it. She grabs it with her long front legs.

Someday you may have a surprise. You may peek inside a flower. You may see a crab spider waiting for her dinner. But you may not see her right away. For crab spiders are hard to find.

Garden spiders are not so hard to find. Garden spiders are easy to see. A garden spider is black and yellow. She has a big puffy body. If you touch her body, it will feel very soft.

The garden spider spins a beautiful web. She spins her web out of silk. The silk will come out of her body. She has six little spinning tubes in the back of her body. The silk will come out of her six little spinning tubes.

The garden spider can spin her web in about an hour. She will make a zigzag in the middle of her web. She will rest on the zigzag. She will wait for her dinner. She will wait for a grasshopper.

Part of the spider's web is very sticky. If a grasshopper jumps into the web, he will get stuck. He will shake the web. He will shake the web a lot.

The spider will run over to the grasshopper. She will run fast. The grasshopper is stuck. But the spider will not get stuck. She has oil on her legs. The oil helps her run on her sticky web.

The spider will grab the grasshopper. She will bite the grasshopper with her fangs. Poison comes out of her fangs. The poison makes the grasshopper die.

The spider will not chew up the grasshopper. She has no teeth. She will stick her fangs into the grasshopper. She will suck up the grasshopper's blood. Spiders do not chew their food. They suck their food.

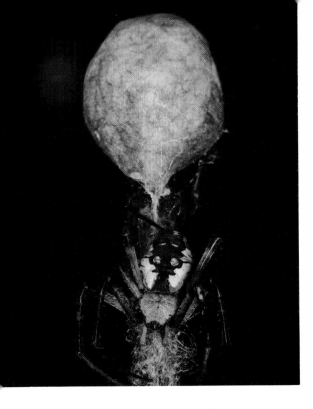

The garden spider lays her eggs in the fall. She covers her eggs with silk to make an egg sac. She hangs her egg sac on a tree. Then she dies.

The baby spiders will come out of the egg sac in the spring. The baby spiders will be very tiny. Each baby wants to find a home. Each baby will crawl up to a high place. Each baby will make a little silk balloon.

The baby spiders make their silk balloons go up into the air. The wind picks up the silk balloon. The baby spiders fly in the air under their silk balloons. The wind takes each baby spider to a new place. When the baby spiders land, they will make webs of their own.

A garden spider is not an insect. A crab spider is not an insect. Spiders are not insects. Spiders have eight legs. Insects have six legs. Spiders do not have wings. Most insects do have wings.

Go for a walk in the fields. If you see a spider, do not be afraid. Be glad the spider is there. Spiders eat insects that hurt plants. They may look creepy. But they help the fields and they help us.

The Firefly

The firefly dances in the fields at night. He shines his light. His light twinkles in the air like a star. It flashes in the sky like a little bit of lightning. That is why some people call the firefly a lightning bug.

The firefly is not really a fly. He is a beetle. In the day, he looks very plain. His back is black or brown or gray. He may have spots. If you turn him over, you can see his light. His light will have a yellow-green color.

The male firefly flies in the sky at night. He tries to find a female firefly. He flashes his light on and off. The female firefly is on the ground. He sends signals to the female. She returns his signals. She flashes her light too.

The firefly's light is a cold light. This is strange. Most light is hot. The light from the sun is hot. The light from a light bulb is hot. But if you touch a firefly's flasher, it will always be cold.

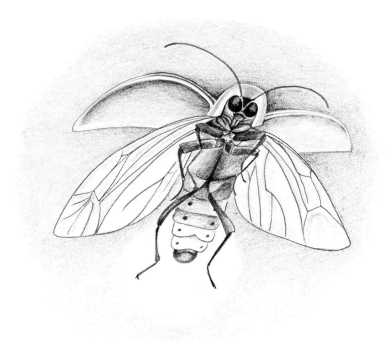

The firefly came out of a tiny egg. When he came out of the egg, he was a larva. A larva is a young insect. A firefly larva and a grown-up firefly do not look at all the same.

A firefly larva is flat. He is brown. He looks like a worm. But he is not a worm. Worms do not have legs at all. But a firefly larva has six legs. His six legs are very tiny.

A larva has fangs too. He has sharp fangs on his head. His fangs look like hooks. He eats with his fangs.

The larva likes to eat snails. He eats snails a strange way. He bites the snail with one of his fangs. He bites the soft part of the snail. This bite makes the snail go to sleep.

Then he bites the snail again with his fangs. Some spit comes out of his fangs. Some juice comes out too. This juice will kill the snail.

You have juice in your stomach. The juice makes your food soft. It makes your food all runny.

The larva has the same kind of juice in his spit. The spit will go into the snail. The spit and the juice make the snail all runny. Then the larva drinks up the runny snail.

After the firefly larva has lived for two years, he will go to sleep for the winter. When he wakes up in the spring, he will be a firefly.

There are many kinds of fireflies in the world. Some fireflies eat snails or worms. Some fireflies eat flower parts. Other fireflies do not eat any food at all. These fireflies do not live for a very long time.

Walk in the fields in the summer. Walk in the fields at night. Watch the fireflies. Watch them flash their lights in the sky. Watch them twinkle!

The Red-Tailed Hawk

The red-tailed hawk sails around in the sky. He sails in circles. He rides on the wind. He hunts for food.

The red-tailed hawk hunts in the day. He sails high in the sky. He looks down in the fields below. He looks for little animals running in the grass.

The hawk has wonderful eyes. He can see much better than you can. When he is up in the sky, he can see a tiny mouse running in the fields. He can see a snake moving in and out of the grass.

When the hawk sees a little animal, he dives down. He dives down to the ground. He grabs the animal with his strong feet.

The hawk's feet are made for hunting. He can grab a mouse or a rabbit with his feet. His feet act like very strong hands.

The hawk has four toes on each foot. Each toe ends with a very sharp claw. The hawk can poke with his claws. He can crush with his claws. He can kill little animals with his claws.

The hawk has a very strong beak. His beak has a hook at the end. The hook is very sharp. The hawk rips his food with his beak. He rips his food into little bits so he can swallow it.

When the hawk eats a mouse, he swallows all the meat. He swallows all the fur too. But the fur will not stay inside of him.

After he eats, many hours pass. Then he spits up the fur. The fur is all stuck together in a hard ball. Every time the hawk eats, he spits up a hard fur ball. The fur ball cleans his insides. But it is not good for food.

The red-tailed hawk makes his nest in a tree. He makes his nest out of sticks. He piles up the sticks between two or three branches. He puts leaves and bark inside of the nest.

When the hawk has a family of babies, he takes care of them. He finds food for them. When he hunts for food, he leaves the nest. He flies out over the open spaces. He flies over the fields.

Sometimes he stops to rest. He rests on a fence or a telephone pole. He stands quietly. He looks around the fields. He looks for animals. If he sees an animal moving, he dives down. He tries to catch it.

The red-tailed hawk is a big strong bird. He has a short tail. His short tail looks like a fan. The feathers on top of his tail have a red-brown color. His wings are long and wide. He sails on the air with his long wide wings.

If you ever see a hawk, watch him fly. Watch him fly high in the sky. Watch him circle around the fields. Watch him dive down and catch a mouse for dinner.

The Meadow Mouse

Lots and lots of meadow mice live in the fields. They run under the grass. They run under the weeds. You may not be able to see them. But they are there.

A meadow mouse is short and fat. Her fur is brown or gray. She has short legs and a short tail. Her head is round. Her little ears are round at the top. Her two little eyes look like little black beads.

Meadow mice have lots of babies.
A young meadow mouse can have
babies when she is four weeks old.
She can have ten babies at a time.
She can have over a hundred babies
in a year!

The meadow mouse makes a little
round nest on the ground. She
makes her nest out of grass. Tall
weeds cover up her nest. It is not
easy to find. The baby mice stay in
the nest for three weeks. Then they
leave.

The meadow mouse is always eating. She eats in the day and she eats in the night. She eats seeds and leaves and grass. She eats bark and roots.

A meadow mouse is very small. She weighs less than a pound. But every day, she eats as much as she weighs. She eats a lot of food for such a little animal.

The meadow mouse stands up when she eats. She stands on her two back legs. She holds her food with her two front legs. She nibbles her food with her big front teeth.

The meadow mouse has four front teeth. She has two front teeth on the top and two on the bottom. Her front teeth are yellow. They are sharp. They keep on growing. A meadow mouse bites a lot of food. If her teeth did not grow, they would wear out!

A meadow mouse is like a lawn mower. She cuts little paths under the tall grass. When she leaves her nest, she runs down one of her paths. She hunts for food. She eats the grass and the seeds that she finds along the way.

In the winter, the meadow mouse lives under the snow. She makes a nest under some old brown grass. But she still has to go hunting. She makes little tunnels in the snow. She runs down her tunnels and hunts for food. She looks for left-over seeds and bits of bark.

The meadow mouse must always hunt for food. But other animals hunt for food too. Many animals like to eat mice for dinner. The poor little meadow mouse has a lot of enemies. A hawk or an owl can fly down from the sky. A fox or a snake can catch her on the ground.

The meadow mouse is a very tiny animal. She is a very busy animal. Her life is always in danger. But she has a lot of babies. So if something happens to her, there will always be other little meadow mice running in the fields.

The Monarch Butterfly

Many people like butterflies. Butterflies are beautiful insects. They look like flowers flying in the sky.

Butterflies come in many colors. They can be black and yellow like a tiger. They can be blue or white or brown.

The monarch butterfly is bright orange and black. You can see him flying over fields and gardens in the fall. The monarch butterfly flies slowly. He is not afraid of birds. Birds do not like to eat monarch butterflies. Monarchs do not taste good to birds.

The monarch butterfly likes to drink juice. He gets his juice from flowers. The flower juice is called nectar.

The monarch has a very long tongue. Most of the time, the monarch rolls up his tongue under his head. When the monarch wants to eat, he unrolls his tongue. He sticks his tongue into the flower. He sucks up nectar with his tongue. His tongue is like a straw.

The monarch can not taste nectar with his tongue. He tastes with his feet. He can taste sweet things with his feet. He can taste sweet things when he steps on to a flower. If a flower is not sweet, he will not drink the nectar.

The monarch has two feelers on top of his head. His feelers help him to find food. His feelers are like thin little fingers. He can feel things with his feelers. He can smell things with his feelers too. He can smell flowers.

The monarch was not so beautiful when he was born. He did not always have orange and black wings. Once upon a time, he was a caterpillar.

A monarch caterpillar is not orange and black. He is yellow and black and white.

The monarch caterpillar came out of a little green egg. The egg was on the bottom of a leaf. It was on a milkweed leaf.

The monarch caterpillar likes to eat milkweed leaves. He has two sharp jaws. His two jaws move from side to side. He cuts the milkweed leaves with his sharp jaws.

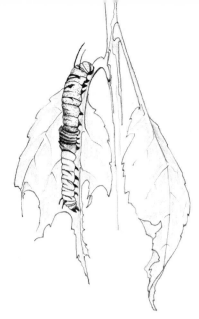

The caterpillar eats and eats and eats. He gets fat. His skin gets tight. His skin pops open. The caterpillar crawls out of his old skin. Now he has a new skin. Every few days, he will pop his skin again. He will pop his skin five or six times. Each time he will get a new skin.

In three weeks, the caterpillar will pop his skin for the last time. He will hang from a milkweed leaf. He will not get a new skin. He will make a thin shell. This thin shell is a chrysalis. The monarch butterfly will grow inside of the chrysalis.

Soon the chrysalis will crack open. The monarch will come out of the chrysalis. He will be very tired. His wings will be very wet.

The wet butterfly will rest. He will pump blood into his wings. His wings will get strong. They will get dry. Then he will be able to fly.

Most butterflies die at the end of the summer. But the monarch will not die. He will live for a whole year. He will fly south for the winter.

Hundreds and hundreds of monarchs fly south in the fall. The flying monarchs look like an orange cloud. They fly for many days. They want to get to a warm place. They fly to a place in California or Mexico.

The monarchs have special trees in California and Mexico. Some people call these trees butterfly trees. The monarchs go to these trees every winter. They hang from these trees. Sometimes you can see hundreds of butterflies hanging on just one tree. Each tree looks like it is full of orange leaves.

Look for monarch butterflies. In the late summer, you can see monarchs in the fields and the gardens. In the fall, you can see monarchs flying south. Keep your eyes open. One or two or ten monarchs may fly right over your head!

49

The Honeybee

Buzz, buzz, buzz. The honeybees buzz in the fields. They buzz around the flowers. They buzz around the dandelions and the white clover. Buzz, buzz, buzz.

Honeybees live in a hive. They live in a hive with thousands of other bees. The hive is made of wax. It has thousands of little rooms. Each little room looks like this: ⬡

The hive can be in a tree or in a box. Three kinds of bees live in the hive. They are the queen bee, the drone bees and the worker bees.

There is one queen bee. The queen bee is the biggest bee. The queen stays in the hive. She lays thousands of eggs. She lays her eggs in many of the little rooms.

There are two or three hundred drone bees in the hive. The drone bees are all males. The drone bees do not work.

The worker bees are females. They are the bees that you see in the fields. They are the bees that buzz around the flowers. The worker bees make all the honey.

Some of the worker bees work in the hive and some work in the fields. A field bee will go out and hunt for flowers. She can smell the flowers. She has two thin feelers on her head. She smells the flowers with her feelers.

She can see the flowers too. She can see colors. She can see the color blue best of all. She can see green and yellow too. But she can not see red. Most of the time she stays away from flowers that are red.

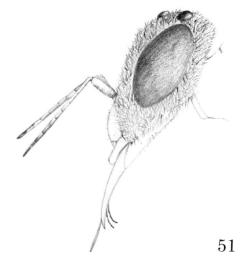

A bee has a tongue. When she finds a flower, she sticks her tongue down into it. She sucks up the flower juice. The flower juice is called nectar.

A bee has two stomachs. She has a big stomach and a little stomach. Her little stomach holds her food. Her big stomach is called a honey bag.

When the bee sucks up nectar, it will go to her honey bag. She will suck nectar from a lot of flowers. She will hold all the nectar in her honey bag.

The honeybee has hairs all over her body. She has hairs on her legs too. Flower dust sticks to all her hairs. This yellow flower dust is pollen.

The honeybee has long stiff hairs on her back legs. The long stiff hairs curve like this: They make a basket. The honeybee has a basket on each back leg. She will brush off all the pollen on her body. She will put this pollen in her two baskets.

When the field bee returns to the hive, she is full of pollen and nectar. Her pollen baskets are full. Her honey bag is full too. First she gives her nectar to a house bee. A house bee is a worker bee who works in the hive. The house bee stores the nectar in one of the little rooms.

Next she empties out her pollen baskets. She pushes the pollen out of her baskets. She pushes it into another little room. Then she flies back out into the fields.

The honeybees all work together. They help each other. They even talk to each other. They talk by doing a dance.

When a field bee finds a lot of sweet flowers, she flies back to the hive. She dances. If the sweet flowers are close to the hive, she dances in circles. If the flowers are far away from the hive, she dances another way. She wags her tail. She dances in the shape of an 8.

The other field bees watch the dance. If they watch carefully, they will be able to find the sweet flowers too. They will know *where* to go. They will know *how far* to go. It is just like magic!

The house bees all stay in the hive. They feed the baby honeybees. They feed the babies pollen and nectar. They mix the pollen and nectar together. They make bee bread. The baby honeybees eat the bee bread.

Each house bee is a young bee. The young bees all work in the hive. They clean the rooms in the hive. On hot days, they fan the hive. They move their wings very very fast. They keep the hive cool. Some of the nectar has turned into honey. If the hive gets too hot, the honey will melt. That is why the young honeybees fan the hive.

When the young bees get a little older, they work as policewomen. They do not let any strange bees into their hive. A strange bee will not have the same smell. The policewomen will push the strange bee away. If the strange bee will not go away, they will sting her. They will kill her.

Every worker bee has a stinger. She will sting when she is afraid. She will sting when she is very mad. But she can only sting one time. After she uses her stinger once, she will die.

A honeybee's stinger has little hooks at the end. When she sticks her stinger into an animal or a person, her stinger comes out. When this happens, some of her insides come out too. Then she can not live.

A worker bee has a busy life. After she works as a house bee, she becomes a policewoman. After she works as a policewoman, she becomes a field bee.

Next time you eat some honey, think of a honeybee. Think of a honeybee flying in the fields. Think of a honeybee sucking nectar from a flower. Think of a honeybee who is making bee bread. Think of a honeybee who is fanning the hive.

Honeybees are all very busy workers. They all work together. They make lots and lots of sweet honey. And some of this sweet honey has been made just for you.

CREDITS

Designed by Gale William Ikola and Cyril John Schlosser
Illustrated by Maarja Roth-Evenson

Photo Credits

Paul Beard/Tom Stack & Associates: 49 (upper right)
Les Blacklock: 6-7, 21 (lower right)
A. Blueman/Tom Stack & Associates: 30
Robert P. Carr: 11, 42
Robert Carr/Tom Stack & Associates: 12-13
Perry Covington/Tom Stack & Associates: 24
John Ebeling/Tom Stack & Associates: 43 (right)
Larry House/Tom Stack & Associates: 21 (upper left)
Wallace Kirkland/Animals Animals Enterprises: 49 (left)
Wallace Kirkland/Tom Stack & Associates: 35
Bill Noel Kleeman/Tom Stack & Associates: 52, 53
Earl Kubis/Tom Stack & Associates: 25, 50
C. Kussner/Tom Stack & Associates: 32
Glenn Maxham, Maxham Films, Inc.: 29
L. David Mech: 14
Robert W. Mitchell/Tom Stack & Associates: 51
Tom and Ceil Ramsey, TCR Productions: 22
Cyril A. Reilly: 26-27
Lynn L. Rogers: cover, 17, 20, 36, 37, 38 (both), 39, 40, 43 (upper left)
Tom Stack/Tom Stack & Associates: 9
John Steel/Animals Animals Enterprises: 47
Lynn M. Stone: 16, 19, 28, 31, 44-45, 48

INDEX